Laughter, Silence and Shouting

KATHY KEAY read English and Education at Oxford and worked as a freelance writer, editor and journalist, giving workshops and seminars in the UK, the USA, India, Africa and South Africa.

The author of eight published titles, she is currently studying for a doctorate in women's spirituality at the University of Bristol.

Laughter, Silence and Shouting

an anthology of women's prayers

COMPILED BY KATHY KEAY

HarperCollins*Publishers*

HarperCollins*Publishers*
77-85 Fulham Palace Road, London W6 8JB

First published in Great Britain
in 1994 by HarperCollins*Publishers*

1 3 5 7 9 10 8 6 4 2

A catalogue record for this book is
available from the British Library

Hardback ISBN 0 551 02889-0
Paperback ISBN 0 551 02824-6

Phototypeset by Harper Phototypesetters Limited,
Northampton, England
Printed and bound in Great Britain by
HarperCollinsManufacturing Glasgow

For LARA with love

Contents

Contents

Our Daily Lives

Who Am I?

Relationships

Other People, Other Places

Work

Justice and Peace

Ages and Stages

Daring to Believe

God Comes to Us

Out of the Depths: Suffering and Death

Resurrection: Hope Restored

Together We Seek the Way

Introduction

Prayer is honest communication: with oneself and with God. That is why I have called this anthology *Laughter, Silence and Shouting*.

Like many before me, in every age and every faith, I have written down my thoughts in the form of prayers when from the depths and heights of momentary experience I have needed to cry out and articulate my deepest longings and fears, hopes and dreams.

This prayer collection was written before and after the birth of my first child, Lara, and soon after the diagnosis of an inoperable breast tumour; it reflects the personal and worldwide concerns of women from biblical times to the present day who know similarly what it means to call upon God, sometimes in great pain and desperation, sometimes with joy and sometimes with a deep cry on behalf of others and for the world in which we live.

The contributions in this volume are a mixture of the known and much loved prayers of women such as Julian of Norwich and Mother Teresa, and the unknown. Some were written several centuries ago, whilst others are quite recent expressions of the newly found freedom many women feel as they strive to formulate their own spirituality. They span not only centuries but continents and whilst the language in which they are written may reflect the age and sentiments in which they live, the themes are remarkably similar: love and longing, faith and doubt, the quest for personal identity and meaningful work; the paradox of suffering, the outrage at global injustice and the ongoing search for God in the midst of life's enigmas – all are expressed with the same passion and vitality.

I hope this anthology will encourage you, the reader, as much as compiling it has encouraged me, to pray honestly from the heart, and inspired by the rich variety of images used by others, to write your own prayers. For it is as we seek to communicate with ourselves and God in this way that our world, our daily lives and relationships, can be transformed. In the words of Elizabeth Jennings.

> Prayer yet could be a dance.
> But still a cross. I offer small heartbreak
> Catch grace almost by chance.

Prayer is not the privilege of a few, it is an instinct deep within us, waiting to be expressed, for there is Someone who will hear us.

Kathy Keay
Great Linford
September 1993

Before Prayer

I weave a silence on my lips,
I weave a silence into my mind,
I weave a silence within my heart.
I close my ears to distractions,
I close my eyes to attentions,
I close my heart to temptations.

Calm me O Lord as you stilled the storm,
Still me O Lord, keep me from harm.
Let all the tumult within me cease,
Enfold me Lord in your peace.

CELTIC TRADITIONAL

God Of Many Names and Faces

Teach Us to Know and Love You

O God of a thousand names and faces,
Mother and Father of all life on earth,
You who live in the cells of all life,
Teach us to know and love you.

Lady of Peace, of Love, of Wisdom,
Lord of all the stars and planets,
Best consoler, inward guest,
Teach us to know and love you.

Giver of gifts and light of our hearts,
Fill the inmost depths of our hearts,
And teach us to know and love you.

Wash what is soiled, heal what is wounded,
Bend what is rigid, warm what is frigid,
And teach us to know and love you.

Restore to us our humanness,
And teach us to know and love you.

SHARON OWENS

Many Faces I Have Thought Were You

Many faces I have thought were you . . .
  The judging father
    successful, demanding
      expecting excellence
     asking that I earn approval
      that I deserve attention
        . . . hoping for his love.

Many faces I have thought were you . . .
  The caring mother
    martyred and all giving
      self-sacrificing
    always thinking of others
      her way the only way
        . . . longing for her love.

Many faces I have thought were you . . .
  A comforting friend
    to be depended on
      nurturer and guide
    with me in the desert
    walking through the valleys
      and long-forgotten paths
        . . . seeking love together.

Many faces I have thought were you . . .
  The giver of life and law
    all knowing
     all being
      all creating
    all seeing
       ever watchful
        even in the darkness of the night
        . . . afraid of your love.

Many faces I have thought were you . . .
  The tragic human figure
   loving . . . hurting
    angry . . . sad
  not spared the death of a son
   but one with us in suffering
       . . . needing to be loved.

Many faces I have thought were you
  all of them . . . and none.

MARY ELLEN GAYLORD

African Prayer

O love and hatch us
Wondrous hen!
We dwell in thy kingdom
Our hen of heaven.

Bakerwoman God

Bakerwoman God,
I am your living bread.
Strong, brown Bakerwoman God,
I am your low, soft and
being-shaped loaf.
I am your rising bread, well kneaded
by some divine
and knotty pair of knuckles,
by your warm, earth hands.
I am bread well kneaded.

Put me in your fire,
Bakerwoman God,
put me in your warm, bright fire.
I am warm, warm as you from fire.
I am white and gold,
soft and hard,
brown and round.
I am so warm from fire.

Break me, Bakerwoman God.
I am broken under your caring Word.
Bakerwoman God,
remake me.

ALLA BOZARTH CAMPBELL

You, O Eternal Trinity

You, O Eternal Trinity, are a deep sea, into which the
more I enter, the more I find, and the more I find, the
more I seek. The soul cannot be satisfied in your abyss,
for she continually hungers after you, the Eternal Trinity,
desiring to see you with the light of your light.

As the hart desires the springs of living water, so
my soul desires to leave the prison of this dark body and
see you in truth.

O abyss, O Eternal Godhead, O sea profound, what
more could you give me than yourself? You are the fire
that ever burns without being consumed; you consume
in your heat all the soul's self-love; you are the fire
which takes away cold; with your light you illuminate me
so that I may know all your truth. Clothe me, clothe me
with yourself, Eternal Truth, so that I may run this
mortal life with true obedience, and with the light of
your most holy faith.

CATHERINE OF SIENA (1347–86)

I It Am

I it am: the might and the goodness of the Fatherhood.
I it am: the wisdom and the kindness of Motherhood.
I it am: the light and the grace that is all blessed love.
I it am: the Trinity. I it am, the Unit.
I it am: the high Sovereign Goodness of all manner of things.
I it am: that maketh thee to love.
I it am: that maketh thee to long.
I it am: the endless fulfilling of all true desires.

JULIAN OF NORWICH

Trinity

In the singing of birds
Is the sound of God.
In the swimming of fish
Is the power of God.
In the moving of beasts
Is the willing of God.
In the heart of humankind
Is the dwelling of God.

In my heart and my head,
In my hands and my feet,
God's Spirit within me
Shall move and shall speak.

EVELYN FRANCIS CAPEL

My Mother

O God my Mother,
You carried me
from conception.
You delivered me
from darkness.
You nourished me
and sustained me.
You let me crawl
and taught me to walk.
You put the first word
into my mouth.
You encouraged me.
You guided me.
You agonized
in my hurts
and my hurtfulness.
You let me go
but never stopped loving,
O God my Mother.

HOSEA II

Communicator God

Communicator God,
thank you that when
talking to you
we are not approaching
a Company Director
but opening our hearts
to Love.

Waters of God

Waters of mountains, waters of God
Cleanse us, renew us, so shabbily shod
Rios de Chile, streams of burnt snow
Melt us, toe us beyond friend or foe.
Currents so fast, pools deep and clear
Tune us, quiet our hearts still to hear.
Lord of the River, God of the Stream
Teach us Your song, our dryness redeem.

CARLA PIETTE
El Salvador

God Our Lover

You draw us to search for you;
you give us clues to your presence in
creation;
We find you in each other's faces,
in the challenge and intimacy of human love.
Yet always you elude our grasp;
familiar and yet always strange,
you both comfort and disturb our
lives.
We surrender all our images of you,
and offer ourselves to your darkness; that you may enable us to
become your likeness
more than we can imagine or
conceive.

JANET MORLEY
Celebrating Women

The Creation

God's World

O world, I cannot hold thee close enough!
Thy winds, thy wide grey skies!
Thy mists that roll and rise!
Thy woods, this autumn day, that ache and sag
And all but cry with colour! That gaunt crag
To crush! To lift the lean of that black bluff!
World, world, I cannot get thee close enough!

Long have I known a glory in it all,
but never knew I this:
Here such a passion is
As stretcheth me apart. Lord I do fear
Thou'st made the world too beautiful this year.
My soul is all but out of me - let fall
No burning leaf; prithee, let no bird call.

EDNA ST VINCENT MILLAY (1892–1950)

Winter

Winter is so beautiful
and the wintry portions of my life
are those which often give birth
to a deeper understanding of who you
created me to be O God.

Winter for me is an eye-opener.
I learn to appreciate
instead of bemoaning,
to delight at the sight
of freshly fallen snow
looking in awe
at the frost-frozen tree limbs
openly rejoicing and celebrating.

Winter gives me more time to explore,
to reach out,
a time to make new plans
with a new ripple of hope
within my soul.

PENNY TRESSLER

Laughter, Silence & Shouting

The Kiss of Spring

Who but You O God can rescue the earth
from the grip of winter?
You take the bare fields, bleak and desolate
and dress them in green,
splashing us with colours,
reminding us that Life comes
through You.
All about me buds are bursting,
I am dwarfed by Your great universe
when spring arrives.

TAMMY FELTON

Wings of the Flying Bird

You are to me, O Lord,
What wings are to the flying bird.

India

Free Flight

Your Easter lesson, Lord,
is not in birds and bees
but seeds and butterflies.
Seeds lie in the ground,
giving themselves completely
in the hope that
new life might emerge
and appear to grow.
Crawling caterpillars, fuzzy worms,
relinquishing their slow
but sure existence
risking all
in the momentary prison
of the cocoon
for the promise of soaring
free flight.
Lord make possible for me
the courage of the lowly worm
that faith of the tiny seed.

ALMA ROBERTS

God Whose Body Is All Creation

God whose body is all creation,
may we come to know you in all the earth
and feel you in our blood;
so will no part of us, or the world,
be lost to your transforming grace.
Amen.

ST HILDA COMMUNITY

A Litany of New Birth

O gracious God of life and birth,
How you labour, how you suffer
to bring forth the new creation!
Indeed you cry out like ,a woman
in childbirth.
And the Spirit groans with you.
But your cries become cries of Joy
As you behold fragile new life
there before you.
All creation waits on tiptoe
for the revealing of your daughters and sons;
We ourselves long to take part in the glorious liberty of your
children.
Who can separate us from the love of God?
Even a mother might forget us,
O God, our God,
How wonderful is your name in all the earth!

RUTH DUCK

Our Daily Lives

Blessed Art Thou

Blessed art thou, O Lord our God, King of the
Universe,
who creates thy world every morning afresh.

HEBREW CONTEMPORARY

Grant that this day and every day,
we may keep our shock of wonder
at each new beauty that comes upon us
as we walk down the paths of life:
and that we may say in our hearts
when horror and ugliness intervene,
Thy will be done.

KATHY KEAY

A Prayer for Each Day's Journey

Touch me, Lord,
With the promise of your dawning,
Prince of the Morning
rising swift and sure.
Breaking through the shadows
Of my fitful sleeping
Bring me to awakening
Of your great love once more.

Touch me, Lord,
With the power of your rejoicing.
Day-star of the noon-time
Rising on the wave
Of our Hope and Glory
In your true light our story,
Unfolding realm of brightness
Your Spirit comes to save.

Be there, Lord,
When my day returns to evening.
Fragrant Rose of Sharon,
Fill this Day of grace
With perfumed oil of gladness
And joy from grief and sadness.
The skies reflect your presence
And the beauty of your face.

Be there, Lord,
When the nightfall veils my vision.
Light in my darkness,
Guide me on the Way.
Bear me on the ocean
In the depths of your compassion.
Bring me safe to harbour
At the closing of my day.

JOAN JOHNSON

My Soul's Healer

Keep me at evening,
Keep me at morning,
keep me at noon.
I am tired,
astray and stumbling,
shield me from sin.

Celtic traditional

May the Power of God this Day

May the power of God this day enable me,
the nakedness of God disarm me,
the beauty of God silence me,
the justice of God give me voice,
the integrity of God hold me,
the desire of God move me,
the fear of God expose me to the truth,
the breath of God give me abundant life.

JANET MORLEY

Inspiring the Commonplace

Mother God
Thank you that when
Your Spirit is at work,
She always produces
in the commonplace
something that is inspiring.

KATHY KEAY

Blessing over a Meal Prepared Together

We give you thanks
for this food which is our life,
for the fruits of the earth,
conceived in darkness
rooted in the secret soil.
We offer you our part in the mess of creativity.
We wash, prepare, cook, present;
we eat and taste and enjoy with our bodies;
we clear away the mess.
We embrace with you the chaos that fulfils,
the secret labour that maintains life.

JANET MORLEY

African Grace

The bread is pure and fresh,
the water is cool and clear.
Lord of all life, be with us,
Lord of all life, be near.

Daring to Dance

Lord God,
Dancer of the Universe,
Take my hand
And dare me
To dance with you
Until I am
Out of breath
And rejoicing

Father God, Hold Me Up

Father God,
Hold me up
from my tumblings
When I have no more energy
to crawl;
When all I seem to do
is fall
Scoop me up, Lord,
Hold me secure
Against your chest
until forgetful of my bruises
I can reach out
Once again
And grasp
Life's glittering mobile.

KATHY KEAY

Woman with a Jug

There is a woman,
An old woman, who shuffles along,
With a jug for a pint of beer.
Almost oblivious,
Seeking oblivion.

Her hair is in metal curlers,
Under an old tweed cap.
Her face is the poor face
Of someone drowned in the sea.

She has never been young,
And her mind is dumb;
And she does not see,
She only floats to the surface,
A terrible accusation to me.
A poor, drowned, bloated face,
Floating up from the sea
Of accepted misery.

And I,
Who lower my eyes for shame
As I go by,
Am more ashamed,
Because I wonder why,
Despair,
Troubles to curl her hair.

CARYLL HOUSELANDER

Invitation

Spirit of the gentle breeze
Breathe on me now;
Still my churning heart
And troubled mind;
Curl my hair softly
With your finger
Until calmed
I am able to believe
In your undying love
Once more.

In the Garden

Here you speak to me
Most clearly
Amidst this
Sea of green
Bedded with pinks and purple
So beautiful this year
After several seasons
of slow growth.
Here in the garden
of my planting
And your watering
You assure me that
All will be well.

KATHY KEAY

Turn Over Gently

Turn over
Gently
My dry, cracked soil.
Just a little,
A little at a time.
Let it breathe
In the cooling air of autumn
And then be watered
By Your life-giving rain.

KATHY KEAY

In This Place

Find a sense of
Church
Community
Communion

Hear a call to
Loving Kindness
Compassion
Unity

Know a time for
Believing
Supporting
Upholding

Recognize a feeling of
Openness
Integrity
Truthfulness

Expect a movement to
Encourage
Include
Forgive

Laughter, Silence & Shouting

Experience a house for
Prayer
People
God

Inhabit a haven for
The weak
The Peacemakers
The Spirit

MAUREEN FARRELL FCJ

Written for the dedication of the
Church of Christ the Cornerstone,
Milton Keynes where Sister Maureen
was City Centre chaplain

(1987-1993)

Rhythm of the Eternal

We thank you, God, for the moments of fulfilment:
the end of a hard day's work
the harvest of sugar cane,
the birth of a child,
for in these pauses
we feel the rhythm of the eternal.

Prayer from Hawaii

Who Am I?

Clarify

Clarify me, please,
God of the galaxies,
Make me a meteor,
Or else a metaphor

So lively that it grows
beyond its likeness and
Stands on its own, a land
That nobody can lose.

God give me liberty
But not so much that I
see you on calvary,
Nailed to the wood by me.

ELIZABETH JENNINGS

Kiss Sleeping Beauty Goodbye

O God,
I feel I have been
Sleepwalking
My way through life;
Waiting in
No woman's land
For something significant to happen;
For someone to come
And lead me to
The Real Life.
Alone
I have felt insignificant;
Unable to take control
Of my own life;
Not sure of what my life is.
Help me to wake up
And measure
My present realities;
Who I am
Where I am
And what I can be;
To kiss Sleeping Beauty goodbye
Once and for all
As I learn
To put my trust
In You.

Inspired by MADDONA KDBENSCHLAG

Betrayal

Judas the disciple of Christ,
Judas the betrayer of Christ,

Judas who repented for his sin,
Judas who paid for his sin
With his own life.

Can we ever understand or know
The violence and passion of this man –
The violence of his intention
And the passion of his love?

Perhaps more than any other
He recognized Jesus as Messiah;
If he did, how could he believe
The Messiah could die?

Can we ever understand or know
Why Judas was Judas?
And how to deal with him within our own hearts?

NALINI JAYASURIYA
Sri Lanka

Mary's Lament

O God,
when I am tempted to doubt
to rage
to despair
Tempted to think
there's no place
for me anywhere;
When I am tempted to rebel
and crave
after a love
nearer, more tangible
and negotiable
than Yours
Woo me,
Rescue me
and establish me
Once more in the safety of
Your everlasting Love.

Mary's Lament II

Now amidst the pain
Now amidst the aloneness
When depression comes in
like a flood;
When tears flow -
Now I love you, Lord,
Now I long to know you,
My God.
Thankful for all the blessings
of life
so thankful
when I am
so undeserving.

KATHY KEAY

In Temptation

When the Evil Inclination
whispers in my ear
let me serve Thee with it.

HASIDIC

Love's Credo

I believe in the integrity of communication,
The mutual freedom to share all
That burdens our hearts
And all spontaneous joys.

I believe in the shared agony
Of mutual acceptance and growth.
The destruction of personalized
Romantic images
Of who we are not.

The reality of who we are
In all our imperfections
And glory.
Not always excited by
The rainbow challenges of
God's amazing world.
Often overcome,
Unattractive
And heart-beaten.

I believe in the burning
Redemptive
Touch of Love
Exposing, restoring
And comforting;
Inspiring us
With courage to be
Gloriously –

KATHY KEAY

Give Me Neither Poverty Nor Riches

Give me neither poverty
nor riches
Lest in my poverty I steal and dishonour Thee
or in my riches I forget Thee.

The Book of Proverbs

Fellowship of Strangers

My poverty
is the permanent lack
of anyone permanent
in my life
whom I can love and touch and rest in.
Dressed in fine clothes,
no one sees
the desert of my heart
and the agony of hungers permanently unfulfilled.
And after all those years
of singing outdated
fond, familiar hymns
I still sit solo
aware of the spaces
in the pew
As in this Fellowship of Strangers
my heart once more
reaches out to You.

Single Woman's Lament

Perfection

To be perfect
even as your Father in Heaven
is perfect . . .

How, O God, am I to understand
the word?
Perfect and pure in heart?
What means pure?
Pure, pure,
Pure apple juice!
I begin to sense a clue.
Pure apple juice is made
from the whole apple;
bruises, blemish, skin, core -
the whole imperfect works.
Pure apple juice is not
pasteurized, refined,
filtered, nonentity!
Bruises, blemishes, skin and core.

To be perfect is to be
whole, a paradox
Even as our Father in Heaven . . .

MARY CAROLINE RICHARDS

Twentieth-Century Woman's Prayer

Communicator God,
when I come to you
with deep concerns
you never silence me.
And when I risk
telling you
my most immediate thoughts
and fears
you do not patronize
or brush me aside.
But you are God
and not man
and it is often with men
that I have to deal.
Help me
in all my dealings with them
to remember
that they too
have need to communicate
underneath their
fragile ego and patched-up
broken heart
and that it is before you
not them
that I stand ultimately
and find my true worth.

ANON

Song

I scan you on the figured page
in tales of every distant age
and chant you in a holy song
but yet I hear, I see you wrong

I am so small
you are so all

and I would scent you in a flower
that flares and fails from hour to hour
and count your liberality
in berries bright upon the tree

but they are small
and you are all

or might I feel you in the sky
your cloudwind lifts my soul so high
or might I taste you in the spring
new-risen, cleanly carolling

I am so small
you are so all

but narrow is my inward sight
I do not spell your meanings right
and guttering my outward gaze
I do not steady trace your ways

my steps are small
to map your all

then break me wide your raging word
in flintstruck light from darkness stirred
and break me wide your dancing love
that soars the hawk, that swoops the dove

I am so small
you are so all in all

VERONICA ZUNDEL

Womb of God

Transforming womb of God
Conceive in us;
Create in us;
Create anew Life:
Faith, the confidence to bear
Hope, continuously expectant
Love, the true beginning.

SALLY DYCK
*written for the graduate school of
Ecumenical Studies, Bossey 1978*

Relationships

Thank You, Lord

Thank you, Lord,
for loving me
when I am my most
unlovable.
Give me love enough
to love others
as you love me.

Friend of the Friendless

Lord God,
Friend of the friendless,
thank you
for our friends.
Help us to be faithful
in loving those
you have brought into our lives.
Keep us free from
needless distractions
and excessive business
so that we can give
our best energies
in nurturing friendship
with them
and with you.

KATHY KEAY

Strong Friendships

Let our friendships be strong, O Lord,
that they become a blessing to others . . .
Let our friendships be open, O Lord,
that they may be a haven for Others . . .
Let our friendships be gentle, O Lord,
that they may bring peace to others . . .
for Jesus' sake, Amen.

C. HERBERT

Confession

O Lord God, we confess
that we are sometimes deliberately unkind to other people.
Forgive us and help us to show them your love.

Laughter, Silence & Shouting

Broken Friendships

Dear God,
Lover of us all,
do not let me go down into the grave
with old broken friendships unresolved.
Give to us and to all with whom
we have shared our lives
and deepest selves
along the Way,
the courage not only to express anger
when we feel let down,
but your more generous love
which always seeks to reconcile
and so to build a more enduring love
between those we have held dear
as friends.

KATHY KEAY

Before Birth: A Waiting Prayer

Here, Lord,
We await your gift of life.
Grown in secret
Now in ripeness
Full fruited
Ready to be received.

Lord, we long for our child,
Borne out of covenant love
Nurtured in love, hope, forgiveness,
Received as gift, blessing, joy.

Release in her abundant grace,
Enjoyment of all that earth affords,
Gentleness to those whose way has been hard,
Patience, kindliness and faith.

We receive, nurture and set free your gift,
Not only our child, but yours,
Yours to enjoy and delight in,
Ours to marvel at your generosity.

Lord of all the living
God of the uncreated and yet to be
Create in us community
As we await your gift.

BARROWBY

Hope Reborn: To My Daughter

Sleep gently, baby, dream your little dreams,
While I watch your face with love, and wonder
What the future holds in store for you.
Let life be kind to you I pray,
All your days.

Let love be your guide in your lifetime,
Love of God, Love of Life and Humanity.

Learn compassion, gentleness and truthfulness,
And have the courage to be just yourself,
All your lifetime.

K. McLAUGHLAN
Iona Community

Birthday Prayer

Soar, Child, soar.
Soar to the bosom of your Father
From the birthing of your Mother.

Grasp, my little one,
The warm hands of Jesus
To love and guide you
Day by day.

Feed, my darling,
On the milk of the Spirit.
God's word and Presence
In our world today.

Be held,
Be free,
Be warmed and fed.

God, Father, Son and Spirit
Be to thee and me
Our clothing, guide, sustainer,
Triune lover since eternity.

BARROWBY

For My Children

On this doorstep I stand
year after year
and watch you leaving

and think: may you not
skin your knees. May you
not catch your fingers
in car doors. May
your hearts not break.

May tide and weather
wait for your coming

and may you grow strong
to break
all webs of my weaving.

EVANGELINE PATERSON

A Little Song

If I were a gypsy,
You - a country gent -
I'd sing to you
Parting and greeting.
If I were a dew drop,
You - a tallish weed -
I'd fall upon you
Every evening.
If I were a river,
You - a bitter ocean -
I'd wash out bitterness
With every motion.
If our families started a royal feud,
I'd run away, dearest,
Barefoot, to you.
If I had in this world
A little more time,
You'd break through to me,
You'd find a way,
As for one last meeting,
request it of God.
They tell me he's friendly,
He can help, they say.

IRINA RATUSHINSKAYA
Shizo

For He Who Would Marry a Childless Woman

O God –
This man's love is awesome!
Who can so deny the inbuilt urge
Of seed to multiply
And trust that You have something else
That needs his fathering, conceive
And bring to birth a shadow-child
With the woman that he loves
More than the treasured dream
Of eager children in his arms
To show the sunflower
And the wild birds to,
To teach the names of stars.

O God –
How can I say I'll make it up to him?
Because I can't.
But I will take his precious gift
Because I never knew a love
So costly and so fine.
It can't be treated lightly.

RO ELDIN WHITE

Forgiveness

Lord, teach us to forgive:
to look deep into the hearts
of those who wound us,
so that we may glimpse,
in that dark, still water,
not just the reflection
of our own face
but yours as well.

SHEILA CASSIDY

Defender God

Defender God,
when people speak falsely
against me,
defend me
and when I speak falsely
against them,
forgive me.

KATHY KEAY

Big Hearts

Give us big hearts, dear God;
big enough to embrace all our sisters
and brothers
especially those in trouble,
whether of their own making or
because of wrongs done to them.
Give us big hearts, dear God;
big enough to acknowledge our own weakness
before pointing the finger at others;
big enough to be humble
when blessed with your good gifts
denied to so many.
Give us big hearts, dear God;
to reach out again and again
to those who cannot help themselves
until hope is restored to them
and we, thorn-beaten and bloodied
allow our loving to become more like yours.

KATHY KEAY

The Sinful Woman

She knelt at his feet
luxuriant black hair
falling gently
caressing his tired feet . . .
fragrant perfume
mingling with dust and dirt
with hair and skin . . .
celebrating a memorial to love.

While eyes
with scorn
disbelief
disgust
see - yet don't see
A woman's faith
celebrating
a memorial to love.

RANJINI REBERA

Last Suppers

Lord Jesus Christ,
Son of the Living God,
Comforter of widows,
Washer of feet,¹
Show us how to care for each other.
Teach us to love as you did:
Unconditionally, unilaterally,
Without fear or favour,
Pride or prejudice.
Give us open hearts and wise minds
And hands that are worthy
To serve in your name.

Send us out

Lord of the Universe
look in love upon your people.
Pour the healing oil of your compassion
on a world that is wounded and dying.
Send us out in search of the lost,
to comfort the afflicted,
to bind up the broken,
And to free those trapped
under the rubble of their fallen dreams.

SHEILA CASSIDY

Other People, Other Places

My Neighbour

I am glad you made my neighbour different from me;
a different coloured skin, a different shaped face;
a different response to you.
I need my neighbour to teach me about you:
She knows all the things I don't know.

MONICA FURLONG

Tender God, Touch Us

Tender God, touch us.
Be touched by us;
make us lovers of humanity
compassionate friends of all creation.
Gracious God, hear us into speech;
speak us into acting;
and through us, recreate the world.

CARTER HEYWARD

Home to the Exile

You are home to the exile
touch to the frozen
daylight to the prisoner
authority to the silent
anger to the helpless
laughter to the weary
direction to the joyful:
come our Lord, come.

JANET MORLEY

A Beggar Woman's Prayer

Lord, I thank you that since with your love you have taken from me all earthly riches, you now clothe and feed me out of the goodness of others, for all that clothes my heart in the desire of possession has become foreign to me.

Lord, I thank you that since you have taken from me the power of my eyes, you now serve me through the eyes of others.

Lord, I thank you that since you have taken from me the power of my hands . . .

Lord, I thank you that since you have taken from me the power of my heart, you now serve me with the hands and hearts of others.

Lord, I ask you to reward them here on earth with your divine love, so that they might beseech and serve you with all virtues until they come to a holy end.

MECHTHILD OF MAGDEBURG (*c. 1210–80*)

Comparisons

I looked, Lord, into Africa
And saw the beauty there;
The insects and the wildlife,
The sunsets and the flowers.

I looked, Lord, into Africa
And saw the suffering there;
The sickness and the poverty,
The famine and the pain.

I looked, Lord, into Britain
And saw the riches there;
The money spent on food and drink
And all the latest 'gear'.

I looked, Lord, at its cities;
The loneliness and fear,
The young and old without a home
Or warming clothes to wear.

I looked, Lord, into Your heart
And saw compassion there
For all your people here on earth,
And love beyond compare.

I looked, Lord, into my heart
And saw indifference there.
O teach me, Lord, to love like You,
To work, to give, to care.

ANN FOAKES

Before Being Deported

The rulers alone decided
That we leave this land
And go across the sea
And the loved one is separated from the beloved . . .

I do not know, O God,
What there is in store for me.
Only let me have your grace
To live with your blessing.

V. MOOKAN
a Tamil woman about to be repatriated
from Sri Lanka during the 1960s

Beatitudes for Disabled People

I

Blessed are you who take time
to listen to defective speech,
for you help us to know that
if we persevere, we can be
understood.

Blessed are you who walk with
us in public places and ignore
the stares of strangers, for in
your companionship we find
havens of relaxation.

Blessed are you that never bids
us 'hurry up' and more blessed
are you that do not snatch our tasks
from our hands to do them for us,
for often we need time rather than help.

Blessed are you who stand beside
us as we enter new ventures, for
our failures will be outweighed
by times we surprise
ourselves and you.

Blessed are you who ask for
our help, for our greatest need
is to be needed.

Blessed are you when by all these
things you assure us that the
thing that makes us individuals
is not our peculiar muscles,
nor our wounded nervous system,
but is the God-given self
that no infirmity can
confine.

MARJORIE CHAPPELL

Blessed are those who realize
I am human
and don't expect me to be saintly
just because I am disabled.

Blessed are those who pick things up
without being asked.

Blessed are those who understand
that sometimes I am weak and
not just lazy.

Blessed are those who forget
my disability of the body
and see the shape of
my soul.

Blessed are those who see me
as a whole person, unique
and complete, and not as a
'half' and one of God's mistakes.

Blessed are those who love me
just as I am without wondering
what I might have been like.

Blessed are my friends
on whom I depend,
for they are the substance and joy
of my life.

MARJORIE CHAPPELL

For Childless Women:
A meditation on Psalm 139

'You knit me together in my mother's womb.'
I may as well add 'spun me, wove me' too,
Or better still, 'embroidered me'.
With care you picked the colour for my eyes,
Decided how much curl to give my hair
And whether it would match well with my skin.
If You knew my mother's womb so intimately
It stands to reason You know mine,
This dusty work-box, unfathomed, wasted,
Now rebellious. What can You see there
From which to fashion anything worthwhile,
Some rusty pins, a few old buttons,
Some faded silk wound round half a letter,
All neglected, left unused too long?
Oh God of miracles, what will You do with these?

RO ELDIN WHITE

God of the Single Parent

Blessed is she who belongs nowhere
because she is with child
but without husband
For You will be her Life Partner.
Blessed is she who has only one pair of hands
to do six tasks at the same time,
urgently.
You will send her unexpected help.
Blessed is she who must provide for all
the needs of her children
and for her own.
You will surely defend her cause.
Blessed is she when the children are in bed
and in the silence of the evening
she craves for adult company.
You will fill her home with your Presence.
Blessed is she when others speak falsely against her
and when she is required to listen to all manner
of dreadful afflictions
which will come upon her children
because they are products of a single-parent household.
You will delight in proving them all wrong
Because she puts her trust in You.

Laughter, Silence & Shouting

For You are the God of the Single Parent
Who knew what it was like
to live against the expectations of society
and said
The Kingdom of Heaven belongs to
such as these.

KATHY KEAY

For Those Who Clean

Dear God, may those who sweep and clean
and take away our rubbish
Be assured of your love and our respect,
for you are the servant of all.

Artists

Thank you, God, for artists;
may they work with honesty and love
and reveal to us
the hidden beauties of our world.

Clouds and the Rainbow

Lord, we thank you for our world,
for its infinite varieties of people,
colours, races and cultures,
for endless opportunities for
making new relationships,
venturing across new frontiers,
creating new things,
discovering new truths,
healing the hurt and the broken.

Forgive us for our narrowness of vision
which sees only the clouds
and misses the rainbow.

As Love Would Make It

Give us, O God, a vision of your world as love would make it;
a world where the weak are protected and none go hungry;
a world whose benefits are shared, so that everyone
can enjoy them;
a world whose different people and cultures live with tolerance
and mutual respect;
a world where peace is built with justice,
and justice is fired with love;
Lord Jesus Christ, give us the courage to build.

AMEN
from Women's World Day of Prayer 1993

Wisdom from the Indians

Every day
to touch the earth with your feet
to warm yourself at the fire
to plunge into the water
to let the air caress you

To know that a day without those four
Sister water Brother fire
Mother earth Father sky
is a lost day

A day in the war
we are waging against everything.

DOROTHEE SÖLLE

Prophecy of an Asian Woman

All the broken hearts
shall rejoice;
all those who are heavy laden,
whose eyes are tired
and who do not see,
shall be lifted up
to meet with
the Motherly Healer.
The battered souls and bodies
shall be healed;
the hungry shall be fed;
the imprisoned shall be free;
all earthly children shall regain joy
in the reign
of the just and loving one
coming for you
coming for me
in this time
in this world.

ASIAN WOMAN'S THEOLOGICAL JOURNAL

God of All

Source and goal
of community,
whose will it is that all
your people enjoy
fullness of life:
may we be builders
of community,
caring for your
good earth
here and worldwide
and as partners with the poor,
signs of your
ever friendly love;
that we may delight in diversity
and choose solidarity
for you are in
community with us
our God for ever.

CHRISTIAN AID

Work

God Give Me Work

God give me work
Till my life shall end
And life
Till my work is done.

WINIFRED HOLTBY
Written on the novelist's grave
at Rudstone, Yorkshire

Work

That which I give my energy to;
which I love
hate
find challenging
demanding
frustrating
rewarding:
This is my work –
that which I must do
on a daily basis
in order to live
and to prove
that I am fully alive.

Lord, thank you that as we work in the world
engaging our best energies
in that which is before us,
you work within us
through that same struggle,
the fabric of our redemption.

KATHY KEAY

To Be a Woman is to Work

They say to me,
as we stop and talk in the street,
'Are you working?'
Well, my Lord,
I'd like to know when
you ever met a woman who
wasn't working?
who wasn't washing and feeding,
fetching and carrying
cooking and cleaning.
We listen to them politicians
on the radio
women as well as men,
but it's us who runs
both home and country
Don't you think, my Lord,
Really?

Sometimes I get discouraged.
Help me and all women workers
the world over

to remember that you're our God
and after all is said and done,
Help us to find our rest in You.

ANON

Daily Prayer

used by workers at Mother Teresa's orphange, Calcutta

Dearest Lord, may I see you, today and every day, in the person of your sick, and whilst nursing them, minister unto you. Though you hide yourself behind the unattractive guise of the irritable, the exacting, the unreasonable, may I still recognize you, and say, 'Jesus, my patient, how sweet it is to serve you.'

Lord, give me this seeing faith, then my work will never be monotonous. I will ever find joy in humouring the fancies and gratifying the wishes of all poor sufferers.

Sweetest Lord, make me appreciative of the dignity of my high vocation, and its many responsibilities. Never permit me to disgrace it, by giving way to coldness, unkindness or impatience.

And, O God, while you are Jesus my patient, deign also to be to me a patient Jesus, bearing with my faults, looking only to my intention, which is to love and serve you in the person of each one of your sick.

Lord, increase my faith, bless my efforts and work, now and for evermore.

MOTHER TERESA OF CALCUTTA

Where Are You Leading?

Oh God, you put into my heart this great desire to devote myself to the sick and sorrowful; I offer it to you. Do with it what is best for your service.

You know that through all these twenty horrible years I have been supported by the belief that I was working with you who were bringing every one of us, even our poor nurses, to perfection. O Lord, even now, I am trying to snatch the management of your world from your hands. Too little have I looked for something higher and better than my own work - the work of supreme Wisdom, which uses us, whether we know it or not.

FLORENCE NIGHTINGALE

Christ's Body

Christ has no body now on earth but yours;
yours are the only hands with which he can do his work,
yours are the only feet with which he can go about the world,
yours are the only eyes through which his compassion
can shine forth upon a troubled world.
Christ has no body on earth now but yours.

TERESA OF AVILA

Dilemma

I live for my work;
For the buzz
of being involved
in making things happen
and contact with
so many interesting people.
I live for my work;
For a good salary
which sustains a home of my own,
enough to eat out twice a week
in the company of friends and
to enjoy holidays overseas
twice a year.
I live for my work;
It gives me a good reason for dressing up
and doing overtime.
When I'm not working
there is nothing and no one
Only You, O God
and my therapist,
to help me make sense of things.

PROFESSIONAL WOMAN'S PRAYER

Spinning Tops

How strange -
we are all so ardent in our piety
so careful not to slip up
so intent on making our individual lives
count in the scheme of things
tyrannized by overful diaries
driven by the echo of our 'well done'.
And where does it all lead?

Spinning round like tops
we spiral down before You
in now grubby, tattered clothes
Out of breath.

Deal gently with us, Lord.

KATHY KEAY

Mill Mother's Lament

We leave our home in the morning,
We kiss our children goodbye,
While we slave for our bosses,
Our children scream and cry.
And when we draw our money,
Our grocery bills to pay,
Not a bit to spend on clothing,
Not a bit to lay away.

How it grieves the heart of a mother,
you every one must know;
but we can't buy for our children,
Our wages are too low.

ELLEN MAY WIGGINS, *1929*

Woman Whose Work is Words

Woman whose work is words
what will you do when words are gone?
Grow in silence like the bees?
Find strength in solitude,
listen to wind, water and living things,
hear what God speaks in silence.

Woman who lives by words
what will you do when words are strange?
Listen for a change?
Learn what people mean in other ways,
smile, gesture, weep even,
live with questions and powerlessness.

Woman who cares for words
what will you do when words overwhelm?
Laugh at jargon?
Be angry
when talk and papers oppress people?
Care more for them and remember
the first and last Word
that makes us one.

JAN PICKARD

Justice and Peace

Peace Care Prayer

Joyfully with Jesus
and with those
who love all life
and try to live
new ways of love,
we push the world away from violence
and pull its victim children
forward into love.

CHRISTINE AND JOHN HARDING

Living Creed

We believe in one God, Author of Life,
Creator of the Universe.
We believe in the Son, Jesus Christ Our Lord,
Who came into the world to seek the lost
And to redeem the whole creation.
We believe in the Holy Spirit, the Giver of Life,
Who leads us to all Truth, renewing us
And enabling us to grow
In the likeness of Christ.
Create in us today
Faith, hope and love
So that together we may liberate
Those who are oppressed
And work towards the renewal
Of the whole earth.

ANON

Come, Holy Spirit, Renew the Whole Creation

With humble heart and body, let us listen to the cries of creation and the cries of the Spirit within it.

Come, the Spirit of Hagar, Egyptian black slave woman exploited and abandoned by Abraham and Sarah, the ancestors of our faith (Genesis 16-21).

Come, the Spirit of Uriah, loyal soldier sent and killed in the battlefield by the great King David out of the King's greed for his wife, Bathsheba (2 Samuel 11:1-27).

Come, the Spirit of Jephthah's daughter, the victim of her father's faith, burnt to death for her father's promise to God if he were to win the war (Judges 11:29-40).

Come, the spirit of male babies killed by the soldiers of King Herod upon Jesus' birth.

Come, the Spirit of Joan of Arc and of the many other women burnt at the 'witch trials' throughout the medieval era.

Come, the Spirit of the people who died during the Crusade.

Come, the Spirit of the indigenous people of the earth, victims of genocide during the time of colonialization and the period of Christian mission to the pagan world.

Come, the Spirit of Jewish people killed in the gas chambers during the holocaust.

Come, the Spirit of people killed in Hiroshima and Nagasaki by atomic bombs.

Come, the Spirit of Korean women in the Japanese 'prostitution army' during World War Two, used and torn by violence-hungry soldiers.

Come, the Spirit of Vietnamese people killed by napalm or hunger in the drifting boats.

Come, the Spirit of Ghandi, Steve Biko, Martin Luther King Jr, Oscar Romero and many unnamed women freedom fighters who died in the struggle for liberation of their people.

Come, the Spirit of our brother Jesus tortured and killed on the cross.

Come, redeem, heal.
Renew us and the whole of Your Creation.

CHUNG HYUN-KYUNG
South Korea

God of Fire, God of Light

God of Fire, God of Light,
Are you the God who answers prayers?
Your people are burning and killing each other
But all they want is land, food,
Education and the vote.

God of Fire, God of Light,
Can we talk to you?
Your people used to be killed by men in uniform
But all they wanted was land, food,
Education and the vote.

God of Fire, God of Light,
Are you listening to us?
Your people are being systematically destroyed
By the faceless strategy of
'Low intensity conflict'
But all they want is land, food,
Education and the vote.

God of Fire, God of Light,
Are you watching over us?
Yes! You are holding up the Light
For us to see the Truth.

God of Fire, God of Light,
You are our Energy, you are our Light.

HEATHER GARNER
South Africa

African Women

You, African women, yes, you
with your ebony black complexion;
You African women
the mother of a wonderful continent:

Like any other woman in the world
you have lived in ignorance,
you have lived amid untold sufferings,
you have known submission,
you have known humiliation,
you have known slavery
and you have sought your freedom.

Rejoice, for you have been heard,
you, with your black ebony complexion;
God has heard your cry and lifted up his countenance upon you;

O African woman,
shed the yoke you have been bearing
from the beginning of time;
put on again the dignity by which God created you
in His image and stand proud - proud to be a woman,
the mother of the black continent.
Like any other woman in the world, perform your role
as a woman giving life through her blood;
fulfil your destiny, you African woman,
in dignity, justice and peace.

RACHEL JAMES MOUKOKO
Iona Community

The Power of Hope

Nailed to a cross because you would not
compromise on your convictions.
Nailed to a cross because you would not
bow down before insolent might.
My Saviour, you were laughed at,
derided, bullied and spat upon
but with unbroken spirit,
Liberator God, you died.

Many young lives are sacrificed
because they will not bend;
many young people in prison for following your lead.
Daily, you are crucified,
my Saviour, you are sacrificed
in prison cells and torture rooms
of cruel and ruthless powers.

The promise of Resurrection,
the power of hope it holds,
and the vision of a just new order
you proclaimed that first Easter morning.
Therefore, dear Saviour, we can affirm
that although bodies are mutilated and broken,
the Spirit refuses submission.
Your voice will never be silenced,
Great Liberating God.

ARUNA GNANADASON
India

Our Father

Our Father
Who is in us here on earth,
Holy is your name
In the hungry who share their bread and their song.
Your Kingdom come,
A generous land where confidence and truth reign.
Let us do your will,
Bring a cool breeze for those who sweat.
You are giving us our daily bread
When we manage to get back our lands
Or to get a fairer wage.
Forgive us
For keeping silent in the face of injustice
And for burying our dreams.
Don't let us fall into the temptation
Of taking up the same arms as the enemy,
But deliver us from evil which disunites us.
And we shall have believed in humanity and life
And we shall have known your Kingdom
Which is being built for ever and ever.

CENTRAL AMERICA

Daily Bread

Give us this day
our calcium propionate
(spoilage retarder)
sodium diacetate
(mould inhibitor)
monoglyceride
(emulsifier)
potassium bromate
(dough conditioner)
chloramine T
(flour bleach)
aluminium potassium sulphate
(acid baking powder)
sodium benzoate
(preservative)
butylated hydroxyanisole
(anti-oxidant)
mono-isopropyl citrate
(sequestrant), plus
synthetic vitamins A and D.

Forgive us, O Lord,
for calling this stuff
BREAD

J. H. REED

Indifference

I was hungry and you blamed it on the communists;
I was hungry and you circled the moon;
I was hungry and you told me to wait;
I was hungry and you set up a commission;
I was hungry and you said, 'so were my ancestors';
I was hungry and you said, 'We don't hire over-35s';
I was hungry and you said, 'God helps those . . .'
I was hungry and you told me I shouldn't be;
I was hungry and you told me that machines do that work now;
I was hungry and you had defence bills to pay;
I was hungry and you said, 'the poor are always with us'.

Lord when did we see you hungry?

God - Let Me Be Aware!

God - let me be aware!
Stab my soul fiercely with others' pain.
Let me walk seeing horror and stain.
Let my hands, groping, find other hands.
Give me the heart that divines, understands,
Give me the courage, wounded, to fight.
Flood me with knowledge,
Drench me with light.
Please keep me eager to do my share.
God - let me be aware!

MIRIAM TEICHNER

You Say You Know

You say you know
all the days
that were planned
for me.

You knew my
unformed substance
in the womb.

You saw me being
made in secret.

Did you see me
being sexually abused?

Did you hear me call to
you in childhood terror
as evil descended on
me?

Did you know me,
then?

How is it you did not
save me?
Stop it happening -
To me, a vulnerable
child?

How does faith work?
Why did you not rescue
me?

Did you weep when you
saw my pain and shame?

What is faith?

Is the fact that I am a
survivor an indication
of your strength?
that even through all the
terror,
You were there?

And that having come out
of it and survived,
I am a testimony to You?

Even today as I speak
to other victims of sexual abuse,
I talk of love and hope,
for forgiveness and believing in
oneself.

Does that mean you knew
you would bring me through?

continued

I do not understand your ways,
God,
but I am still alive to see your
loving kindness in the land of
the Living.

Prayer of a sexually-abused woman,
based on Psalm 139

All Is Silent

All is silent
In the still and soundless air,
I fervently bow
To my Almighty God.

HSIEH PING-HSIN, China

Our Prayer

Make us keep the sputtering lantern burning
and not to break a wounded reed.
Make us understand
the secret of eternal life
from the pulse of blood in our veins
and realize the worth of a life
from the movement of a warm heart.
Make us not discriminate
the rich and the poor
the high and the low
the learned and the ignorant
those we know well and those we do not know.
Oh!
A human life can't be exchanged for the whole world,
this supreme task of keeping the lives
of sons and daughters of God.
Let us realize how lovely it is
to feel the burdens of responsibility.

a worker of Peace Market, Korea (written during study at night 1977)

Universal Prayer for Peace

Lead us from death to life,
from falsehood to truth.
Lead us from despair to hope,
from fear to trust.
Lead us from hate to love,
from war to peace.
Let peace fill our hearts,
our world, our universe.
Let us dream together,
pray together
work together,
to build one world
of peace and justice for all.

Ages and Stages

God grant me
Serenity to accept the things I cannot change,
Courage to change the things I can,
And wisdom to know the difference.

ANON

Before the beginning Thou hast foreknown the end,
Before the birthday the death-bed was seen by Thee:
Cleanse what I cannot cleanse, mend what I
cannot mend,
O Lord All Merciful, be merciful to me.

While the end is drawing near I know not mine
end;
Birth I recall not, my death I cannot foresee:
O God, arise to defend, arise to befriend,
O Lord All Merciful, be merciful to me.

CHRISTINA ROSSETTI

Explorer God

Explorer God,
You have put within us
a spirit of adventure
to move us beyond
the immediate
and to explore even
our most familiar environment
to its fullest potential.

May each day become an adventure
of people, tasks, places
and responsibilities.
And when I feel grey and lifeless,
may your Spirit remind me that
each day brings
its own gifts
and that the best
is yet to be.

PRAYER OF A WOMAN AT HOME

Laughing, We Endure

(on moving house)

We live for a time secure,
beloved and loving
sure
it cannot last for long,
and when the goodbyes come
again and again,
each like
a little death,
the closing of a door,
laughing we endure.

One learns to live with pain,
One looks ahead
not back,
only before,
and believes
that Joy will come again,
warm and secure.
If only for the now,
O Lord
laughing
we endure.

KATHY KEAY

On Accepting Restrictions

Fly humbly
when you fly;
and walk when you can.

There Will Be Less Some Day

There will be less some day,
much less,
and there will be more.
Less to distract
and amuse;
more to adore;
less to burden and confuse;
more to undo,
the cluttering of centuries
that we might view again
that which star and angels pointed to.
We shall be poorer
and richer,
stripped and free,
when unafraid
we look upon Thee.

The Happiness of Being Alive

Once life has almost been
taken from you,
When for some strange reason
you emerge from death
and blink
with new eyes upon the old
almost forgotten universe,
then you can understand
once more
the value of sea and stars,
of happiness uncontainable,
the sheer relief and delight of being alive
that turns your eyes repeatedly
upwards
with thanksgiving
then straight outward
declaring peace over and over again
to those who with heads bent low
see mud not stars.

KATHY KEAY

Prayer of an Ageing Woman

Lord, you know better than I know myself that I am growing older and will some day be old. Keep me from being talkative and particularly from the fatal habit of thinking that I must say something on every subject and on every occasion.

Release me from craving to straighten out everybody's affairs. Make me thoughtful but not moody; helpful but not bossy. With my vast store of wisdom, it seems a pity not to use it all, but you know, Lord, that I want a few friends at the end. Keep my mind from the recital of endless details - give me wings to come to the point.

I ask for grace enough to listen to the tales of others' pain. But seal my lips on my own aches and pains - they are increasing, and my love of rehearsing them is becoming sweeter as the years go by. Help me to endure them with patience.

I dare not ask for improved memory but for a growing humility and a lessening cocksureness when my memory seems to clash with the memories of others. Teach me the glorious lesson that occasionally it is possible that I may be mistaken.

Keep me reasonably sweet. I do not want to be a saint - some of them are so hard to live with - but a sour old woman is one of the crowning works of the devil!

Give me the ability to see good things in unexpected places, and talents in unexpected people. And give me, O Lord, the grace to tell them so.

Attributed to a seventeenth-century nun

Silly Devotions

From silly devotions
and from sour-faced saints,
good Lord, deliver us.

TERESA OF AVILA

Lord Grant That My Last Hour

Lord grant that my last hour
may be my best hour.

Old English prayer

God Be In My Head

God be in my head,
And in my understanding;
God be in my eyes
And in my looking;
God be in my mouth,
And in my speaking;
God be in my heart,
And in my thinking;
God be at my end,
And at my departing.

Indian traditional

Last Lines

No coward soul is mine,
No trembler in the world's storm-troubled sphere:
I see heaven's glories shine,
And faith shines equal, arming me from fear.

O God within my breast,
Almighty, ever-present Deity!
Life – that in me has rest,
As I – undying Life – have power in Thee!

Vain are the thousand creeds
That move men's hearts: unutterably vain;
Worthless as withered weeds,
Or idlest froth amid the boundless main,

To waken doubt in one
Holding so fast by Thine infinity;
So surely anchored on
The steadfast rock of immortality.

With wide-embracing love
Thy spirit animates eternal years,
Pervades and broods above,
Changes, sustains, dissolves, creates and rears.

Though earth and man were gone,
And suns and universes ceased to be,
And Thou wert left alone,
Every existence would exist in Thee.

There is not room for Death,
Nor atom that his might could render void:
Thou - THOU art Being and Breath,
And what THOU art may never be destroyed.

EMILY BRONTË (*1818-48*)
The last lines my sister Emily ever wrote
(note by Charlotte Brontë).

Thanks for Life

I thank Thee, God, that I have lived
In this great world and known its many joys:
The song of birds, the strong, sweet scent of hay
And cooling breezes in the secret dusk.
The flaming sunsets at the close of day,
Hills and the lonely, heather-covered moors,
Music at night and moonlight on the sea,
The beat of waves upon the rocky shore
And wild, white spray, flung high in ecstasy.
The faithful eyes of dogs and treasured books,
The love of kin and the fellowship of friends,
And all that makes life dear and beautiful.
I thank thee too, that there has come to me
A little sorrow and sometimes defeat,
A little heartache and the loneliness
That comes with parting, and the word 'Goodbye',
Dawn breaking after dreary hours of pain,
When I discovered that night's gloom must yield
And morning light break through to me again.
Because of these and other blessings poured
Unasked upon my wondering head,
Because I know that there is yet to come
An even richer and more glorious life,
And most of all, because thine only Son
Once sacrificed Life's loveliness for me –
I thank Thee God that I have lived.

ELIZABETH CRAVEN

I Shall Pass Through

I shall pass through
this world but once.
Any good therefore
that I can do
or any kindness
that I can show
to any human being
let me do it now.
Let me not defer
or neglect it,
for I
shall not pass
this way again.

ANON

Daring to Believe

Be Thou My Vision

Be Thou my vision, O Lord of my heart;
Naught be all else to me, save that Thou art -
Thou my best thought by day or by night,
Waking or sleeping, Thy presence my light.

Riches I heed not, nor man's empty praise,
Thou mine inheritance, now and always;
Thou and Thou only, first in my heart,
High King of Heaven, my treasure Thou art.

High King of Heaven, after victory won,
May I reach heaven's joys, O bright heaven's Sun!
Heart of my own heart, whatever befall,
Still be my Vision, O ruler of all.

MARY BYRNE (*1880-1931*)
Ancient Irish

Dedication

May the mind of Christ my Saviour
Live in me from day to day,
By his love and power controlling
All I do or say.

May the Word of God dwell richly
In my heart from hour to hour,
So that all may see I triumph
Only through his power.

May the peace of God my Father
Rule my life in everything,
That I may be calm to comfort
Sick and sorrowing.

May the love of Jesus fill me,
As the waters fill the sea;
Him exalting, self abasing
This is victory.

May I run the race before me,
Strong and brave to face the foe,
looking only unto Jesus
As I onward go.

KATE BARCLAY WILKINSON (*1859–1928*)

Just as I Am

Just as I am, without one plea
But that Thy blood was shed for me,
And that Thou bidd'st me come to thee,
O Lamb of God, I come.

Just as I am, though tossed about
With many a conflict, many a doubt,
Fightings and fears within, without,
O Lamb of God, I come.

Just as I am, poor, wretched, blind, -
Sight, riches, healing of the mind,
Yea, all I need, in Thee to find,
O Lamb of God, I come.

Just as I am, Thou wilt receive,
Wilt welcome, pardon, cleanse, relieve;
Because thy promise I believe,
O Lamb of God, I come.

Just as I am - thy love unknown
Has broken every barrier down -
Now to be Thine, yea Thine alone,
O Lamb of God, I come.

Just as I am, of that free love
The breadth, length, depth and height to prove,
Here for a season, then above, -
O Lamb of God, I come.

CHARLOTTE ELLIOTT (*1789-1871*)

Voice in My Silence

I believe that God is in me as the sun is in the colour and fragrance
of a flower - the Light in my darkness, the Voice in my silence.

HELEN KELLER

*Helen Keller became blind and deaf in infancy and never experienced
the reality of human speech.*

Love's Faithfulness

You offer comfort
in affliction.
Within the wasteland of
my pilgrim heart
You stand radiant
moving forward,
dustblown through the years
facing every onslaught
wiping every tear
defusing every deception
disarming vanity
confronting pride -
idolatry of every kind.
Seemingly lost amidst unbelief
and the pain and turmoil
of past years
and recent grief,
yet here you stand

With you I emerge
burnt
yet more vulnerable
more real.

KATHY KEAY

Despite All

I must continue
to believe
when you close doors
you open windows
but now all the doors
I've knocked on
have slammed shut
and not so much
as a curtain
is pulled open

You put out all my light
how can you expect me to be
light to the world
when I feel darkest night?

You drain away all my salt
how can you expect me to be
salt of the earth
when I feel dry as mould?

ELLEN WILKIE

Afraid

As I looked
a mist blurred
my mirror vision
my face dissolved
into a cloud of confusion
worries seized my brain
my head seemed to contain
an excessive burden
then your words encouraged me
'Let tomorrow's troubles come tomorrow'
the mist cleared
and I trusted
in You

ELLEN WILKIE

In Weariness

O Lord Jesus Christ
who art as the shadow of a great rock in a weary land,
who beholdest thy weak creatures
weary of labour, weary of pleasure,
weary of hope deferred, weary of self,
in thine abundant compassion,
and fellow feeling with us,
and unutterable tenderness,
bring us we pray thee,
unto thy rest.

CHRISTINA ROSSETTI (*1830–94*)

Advent

We who look ahead
Behold thee coming towards us,
Proclaiming what is
And what shall be.
Strengthen our faith,
Thou who art, who will be
Throughout the times.
Make clear our sight,
Thou who art born for
What is to come.

EVELYN FRANCIS CAPEL

Daring to Believe _____

Advent 1992

The promise of
a new life
is before me
and I
with big belly
on weak hips
struggle
to turn away from
all that has been
towards all
that will be
as I heave myself
upwards
aided only by
Your invisible hands
then release
my full body
once more onto
the clean welcoming
surface of my bed
beckoning sleep,
waiting for
deliverance.

KATHY KEAY

God Comes to Us

Christmas

In the piercing cry of a baby
the blind, naked cry
of a human soul
entering the world
for the first time -
God comes to us
deliberately
vulnerable
and unclothed.

KATHY KEAY

Mary's Song
Luke 1:46-55

My heart praises the Lord;
my soul is glad because of
God my Saviour,
for he has remembered me,
his lowly servant!
From now on all people
will call me happy,
because of the great things
the Mighty God has done for me.
His name is holy;
from one generation to another
he shows mercy to those
who honour him.
He has stretched out his mighty arm
and scattered the proud
with all their plans.
He has brought down
mighty kings from their thrones,
and lifted up the lowly.
He has filled the hungry
with good things,
and sent the rich away
with empty hands.

He has kept the promise
he made to our ancestors,
and has come to the help
of his servant Israel.
He has remembered
to show mercy . . .

Good News Bible

Victory

Down to that littleness, down to all that
Crying and hunger, all that tiny flesh
And flickering spirit – down the great stars fall,
Here the huge kings bow.
Here the farmer sees his fragile lambs,
Here the wise man throws his books away.

This manger is the universe's cradle,
This singing mother has the words of truth.
Here the ox and ass and sparrow stop,
Here the hopeless man breaks into trust.
God, you have made a Victory for the lost.
Give us this daily Bread, this little Host.

ELIZABETH JENNINGS

The Birth of Jesus

Born among the poor on a stable floor,
cold and raw, you know our hunger,
weep our tears and share our anger
yet you tell us more, born among the poor.

Every child needs bread till the world is fed:
you give bread, your hands enable,
all to gather round one table.
Christmas must be shared,
every child needs bread.

Son of poverty shame us till we see
self-concerned how we deny you,
by our greed we crucify you
on a Christmas tree, son of poverty.

SHIRLEY MURRAY
New Zealand

Epiphany

What was invisible we behold,
What was unknown is known.
Open our eyes to the light of grace,
Unloose our hearts from fear,
Be with us in the strength of love,
Lead us in the hope of courage
Along the path of tribulation,
Till the overcoming is attained.

EVELYN FRANCIS CAPEL

Out of the Depths:
Suffering and Death

Lent

Cast down to the depths,
Raise us to uprightness.
Make us stand straight on the earth,
Head high, feet firm, hands free.
Lift us from uncertainty,
Bestow on us our humanity.
Keep us in thy faith
That we fall not away into the gloom.

EVELYN FRANCIS CAPEL

Out of the Depths

Out of the depths I cry to you, O God,
Hear my voice, O God, listen to my pleading.

My voice is weak, O God, my God,
Although it speaks for many.
It is the voice of Sarah, shamed
before her servant,
Barren, and given no worth.

It is the voice of Hagar, abused
by her mistress.
Driven out into the desert with her child.
It is the voice of Rachel, weeping
for her children,
Weeping, for they are all dead.

It is the voice of Mary, robbed
of her humanity.
Woman, yet not woman.
It is the voice of Martha, taught
to be a servant,
challenged to choose for herself.
It is the voice of a nameless woman,
bought and sold,
Then given back to herself.

It is the voice of women groaning in labour,
Sweating in toil, abandoned in hardship,
Weeping in mourning, awakened in worry,
Enslaved in dependency, afraid of their weakness.

Do you hear my voice, O God, my God?
Can you answer me?
The words I hear all speak to me of men.
You said I am also in your image,
You are my father, are you also mother,
Comfort-bringing like the loving arms?

Do you hear my voice, O God, my God?
Can you answer me?
I can sing your song of praise no longer,
I am not at home in this world any more.
My heart is full of tears for my sisters,
They choke my words of joy.

Do you hear my voice, O God, my God?
Can you answer me?
You sent your son, a man, to love me,
But him they killed also.
What is the new life that you promise me?
I DO NOT WANT MORE OF THE SAME.

KATHY GALLOWAY

Waiting

Waiting for you
reminds me
of all other people in the world
waiting:
Those in prison
confined, shut off
waiting for time to pass
or death
to bring release:
Those in pain
maimed by accidents of a physical kind
waiting to be healed back to an active life.
And those with accidents
of another kind:
divorce, unemployment, schizophrenia
the old, the ugly, the lonely
those on the margins
sitting uncomfortably
waiting
for love, for work, for sanity
for respect, for healing
for someone or something to fill the gaps
and soothe the pain
reinforced by time.

continued

I look at the gate, now mended
and firmly closed.
You do not come.
I turn from emptiness to emptiness
O God
yet wonder if You are also waiting
in the shadows?

Waiting Woman's prayer

Jesus is Condemned to Death

Lord, You sit in silence
but it is too late for You to be quiet.
You have said too much.
You have fought too much.
You have challenged everything
that makes us feel secure.
You weren't sensible, you know,
in the way You did things;
You exaggerated and threatened people.
They were bound to catch up with you
in the end.

You called the religious people
'a load of wets'.
You told them that their hearts were
like sewers and that all their rituals
stank to high heaven.

You didn't mix with the right people, Jesus.
You didn't only go and visit
those left to rot in prison cells
and mental hospitals,
You loved them, laughed and sang
with them.
When the rest of us were scared to death
about our own health and safety,
You embraced the AIDS victim
and held him up as an example
of one who knew his need.

You talked with people who felt cheated
by the system and gave them hope;
On the streets, in grotty housing and
down at the dole.
No wonder the authorites were worried.
You sacrificed security for
the life of the homeless,
travelling in often tough places
and spending time with those who needed You
the most.
You spent little time inside religious buildings,
and when you turned over the
'Trinkets for Jesus' stalls,
no wonder they didn't ask you back.

continued

You reduced thousands of years of theology
into one little command:
to love your neighbour as yourself.
How hard that is!
Now they have caught You
but as You stand before the frantic crowd,
You know it is they not You
in whom the Spirit has died.

Help us to follow You, Lord.
We have grown used to the comfort
of other people's praise.
It is not so easy for us
to stand alone
as You did.
Give us courage to go against the crowd
to die to self-interest
and so to overcome
evil in the world today.

from Meditations on Stations of the Cross
written for the Good Friday service at Iona Abbey
Kathy Keay, Easter 1987

_____ *Laughter, Silence & Shouting*

We Without a Future

We, without a future,
Safe, defined, delivered
Now salute You God,
Knowing that nothing is safe,
Secure, inviolable here.
Except You,
And even that eludes our minds
at times.

ANNA McKENZIE

We Did Not Want It Easy, God

We did not want it easy, God,
But we did not contemplate
That it would be quite this hard,
This long, this lonely.
So, if we are to be turned inside out,
And upside down,
With even our pockets shaken
Just to check what's rattling
And left behind,
We pray that you will keep faith with us,
And we with you,
Holding our hands as we weep,
Giving us strength to continue,
And showing us beacons
Along the way
To becoming new.

ANNA McKENZIE

Brokenness:
Who Touched Me?

We all bleed.
we bleed for ourselves –
we each have our private pain.
we bleed for others;
and we bleed for a wounded world.

If we did not bleed for others
in some measure,
would we not be spiritually barren?
unfit for our calling,
incapable of conceiving and nurturing
new life,
forming relationships and caring
communities.

But if the pain takes over
and the bleeding becomes constant
do we not then find that
we have lost touch with our Lord?

He is obscured by the crowd of
our concerns,
the crowd of our activities,
the crowd of our own words.

Jesus, help us to touch you now,
to lay before you
our own and the world's pain.
Help us as we wait in silence
to feel your healing hands
upon us.

MARK 5: 24-34
Consultation of Methodist women ministers
Oxford 1984

No Lamb in the Thicket

When I am spread out
ready for the surgeon's knife
There will be no lamb caught
in the thicket
to spare me.
I see it now
the knife in the shadows –
Down it comes
gouging out my right breast
leaving only an ugly scar
and a deeper, more enduring pain
while they talk of
possible Reconstruction
instead of
complete Liberation
into your Arms of Love.

KATHY KEAY

Shock Me, Rock Me

Shock me
Rock me
Mutilate me
Heal me
If You must,
So that I
Your once beautiful
Now maimed
Half-woman
Will yet dare
To love You
Twice as much.

on contemplating mastectomy
  after breast cancer diagnosis

KATHY KEAY

By His Wounds You Have Been Healed

O God,
through the image of a woman
crucified on the cross
I understand at last.

For over half my life
I have been ashamed of the scars I bear.
These scars tell an ugly story,
a common story,
about a girl who is the victim
of sexual abuse.

In the warmth, peace
and sunlight of your presence
I was able to uncurl
the tightly clenched fists.
For the first time
I felt your suffering presence with me
in that event.

I have known you as a vulnerable baby,
as a brother, and as a father.
Now I know you as a woman.
You were there with me
as the violated girl
caught in helpless suffering.

The chains of fear
no longer bind my heart and body.
A slow fire of compassion and forgiveness
is kindled.
My tears fall now
for man as well as woman.

You were not ashamed of your wounds.
You showed them to Thomas
as marks of your ordeal and death.
I will no longer hide these wounds of mine.
I will bear them gracefully.
They will tell a resurrection story.

ANONYMOUS I PETER 2:24

*Inspired by the figure of a woman, arms outstretched as if
crucified, hung below the cross in a chapel in Toronto, Canada.*

Beauty for Ashes?

You said you would
give me
beauty for ashes,
the oil of joy for mourning,
the garment of praise for
a spirit of heaviness.

I have known all these.

For I am one who has
known the pain of
sexual abuse as an
innocent child.

I am now thirty-five.
Will you bring me beauty
for ashes of a life that should
have been?

The oil of joy for
years of mourning a lost
childhood,
adolescence and adulthood?

Will I be clothed in righteousness?
Will the garment of my being, be
covered in praise -
praise of who I am in You?
Shaking free the guilt of
tormented years?
Will the silence I endure be gone?

And my spirit of heaviness,
clothed in depression,
tranquilizers, alcohol and
pain,
be turned into something
positive?

Dear God,
I am trusting you
to bring something
good out of
this.

Reflections on a sexually-abused child,
BRIDGETTE TAYLOR

Daring to Believe

Lord of Life,
We believe in you.
We believe you lived like us
And we know you died a messy death,
While your friends stood helpless by.
Lord, we believe (don't ask us how)
That you rose again -
Somehow transformed, glorious and immortal,
Yet still yourself.
We dare to believe because of you,
That we too shall rise,
Most wonderfully changed,
Yet still ourselves, to be with you.
Lord, help our unbelief.

SHEILA CASSIDY

Resurrection: Hope Restored

Corn King

Corn King
spring!
leap, leap, Lord of Light;
dance, dance, dear delight.

grain buried deep,
today, tomorrow sleep
then
lightward
larkward
skyward
godward
leap
bright to death.

continued

Broken Corn King harvested,
threshed, ground, milled for bread,
at daylight leap
from your dark sleep
begin
the dance, the dear delight
of yielded sheaves, golden, bright,
a garnered hoard
welcoming the Harvest Lord
while corn-fat valleys shout and sing
honouring
the harvest king;
feasting
the harvest home
with broken bread and one cry: Come!

JENNY ROBERTSON

Reminder

Lord God,
Thank you for giving me back
My life;
For proving your love and faithfulness
In spite of
So much that was against me.
Let it never be said
You are impotent.
Rather remind us that
You are always ready
To help us
Beyond our wildest expectations
If only
We turn to you
In our need,
Whether it be great
Or small.

Hope Restored

Amidst affliction
You have turned round
the pieces
of my life.
Where once there was
too much sky
and cloud,
Now plenty of grass
and a path on which to walk
with steady feet.

KATHY KEAY

After successful cancer treatment

Hannah's Prayer

*(after bearing her son, Samuel, whom she dedicated
to God to serve in the Temple).*

My heart exults in Yahweh,
my horn is exalted in my God,
my mouth derides my foes,
for I rejoice in your power of saving.

There is none as holy as Yahweh,
(indeed there is no one but you)
no rock like our God.

Do not speak with haughty words,
let not arrogance come from your mouth.
For Yahweh is an all-knowing God
and his is the weighing of deeds.

The bow of the mighty is broken
but the feeble have girded themselves with strength.

The sated hire themselves out for bread
but the famished cease from labour;
the barren woman bears sevenfold,
but the mother of many is desolate.

Yahweh gives death and life,
brings down to Sheol and draws up;
Yahweh makes poor and rich,
he humbles and also exalts.

He raises the poor from the dust,
he lifts the needy from the dunghill
to give them a place with princes,
and to assign them a seat of honour;
for to Yahweh the props of the earth belong,
on these he has poised the world.

I SAMUEL 2: 1–8

Resurrection: Hope Restored

Credo

I believe
no pain is lost,
no tear unmasked,
no cry of anguish
dies unheard;
no man or bird
crushed
unseen
without wounded hands
which shaped
the cosmos
reshaping still
the bits and pieces
of who we are
and what
in spite of life's cruel 'accidents'
we yet shall be.

(After my brother's death,
1983)

KATHY KEAY

Stand By Us

Jesus, who was lost and found in the garden,
never to be lost again,
Stand by us in the darkness of our crucifixions,
as the women stood by you.
Die and rise with us in the suffering of the world.
Be reborn with us
as love and hope and faith and endurance
outlast cruelty and death.
Amen.

Disturb and Heal Us

May the God who shakes heaven and earth,
whom death could not contain,
who lives to disturb and heal us,
bless you with power to go forth
and proclaim the gospel.
Amen.

Easter Blessing

JANET MORLEY

Together We Seek the Way

Together We Seek the Way

Loving God
together we seek the way,
helping, watching, learning, leading,
each step forging new links,
each dialogue opening further
the channels of peace and understanding.
We stand poised on the brink of greatness,
drawn by the Spirit into new realms of hope and trust.
The barriers of past centuries
are slowly crumbling.
We pray that the skeletons of division and discord
will be laid to rest,
and that the people of God will be fully mobilized.
For these and all your mercies,
we thank and praise you, O God.

ST HILDA COMMUNITY

Laughter, Silence & Shouting

Ascension Day 1993

You
ascended triumphant
and we still
earthbound
and confused
look up
wondering
at your presence
now absence.

How easily cooled
we are by your departing.
How much we need
you
to be one of us

We travel on
with eyes lowered
bending to soothe
our dusty and blistered feet,
and wait
once more
for the manger.

KATHY KEAY

Call to Worship

O Lord our God,
You are the great God
You are the creator of life;
You make the regions above
and sustain the earth from which we live.
You are the hunter who hunts for souls.
You are the leader who goes before us.
You are the great mantle which covers us.
You are the one whose hands are with wounds.
You are the one whose blood is a living stream.
Today we say thank you, our God
and come before you in silent praise.

Whitsun

Spirit sent from God come us-ward,
Deposit thy flame
Where the Christ-seeking heart awaits.
May light burst from the flame
Burning more courageously
From day to day
Shedding its light of wisdom
From night to night.   EVELYN FRANCIS CAPEL

Life-giving Spirit

Life-giving Spirit
thank you that
your guidance
is not an imposition
of your will
over ours,
wringing all pleasure
and spontaneity
from our lives.
Thank you that
it can come naturally
as like a loving parent
You let us
chart out our own path,
guiding us gently
from behind.   KATHY KEAY

Vige Creatrix Sophia

Rage, Wisdom, and our lives inflame,
so living never rests the same:
you are creative power and art
to blow our mind and wrack our heart.

As fiery gale, as storm of love,
discomfort, burn, all wrong remove,
exposing with your searing light
the lovelessness we keep from sight.

Disrupt and right our unjust ways
with the abrasion of your grace;
while we're your foes let no rest come
till to Christ's love you've brought us home.

You gust and burn through time and space,
and strange your beauty, fierce your face;
disturb our sleep and break our peace;
till Christ's love win, don't, Lady, cease.

Bring us to love the Father, Son,
and you with them, in love as one,
that through the ages all along
this may be our endless song:

Praise to love's eternal merit,
Father, Son and wisest Spirit.

ST HILDA COMMUNITY

A Litany of Women's Power

All: Spirit of Life, we remember today the women,
named and unnamed, who throughout time have used
the power and gifts you gave them to change the world.
We call upon these foremothers to help us discover
within ourselves your power - and the ways to use it to
bring about the Kingdom of Justice and Peace.

We remember SARAH who with Abraham answered
God's call to forsake her homeland and put their faith in
a covenant with the Lord.
We pray for her power of faith.

We remember ESTHER and DEBORAH, who by acts of
individual courage saved their nations.
We pray for their power of courage to act for the greater
good.

We remember MARY MAGDALENE, and the other
women who followed Jesus, who were not believed when
they announced the resurrection.
We pray for their power of belief in the face of
scepticism.

We remember PHOEBE, PRISCILLA, and the other
women leaders of the early Church.
We pray for their power to spread the Gospel and inspire
congregations.

We remember the Abesses of the Middle Ages who kept faith and knowledge alive.
We pray for their power of leadership.

We remember TERESA of Avila and CATHERINE of Siena who challenged the corruption of the Church during the Renaissance.
We pray for their powers of intelligence and outspokenness.

All: We remember our own mothers and grandmothers whose lives shaped ours.
We pray for the special power they attempted to pass on to us.

We pray for the women who are victims of violence in their homes.
May they be granted the power to overcome fear and seek solutions.
We pray for those women who face a life of poverty and malnutrition.
May they be granted the power of hopefulness to work together for a better life.

We pray for the women today who are 'firsts' in their fields.
May they be granted the power to preserve and open up new possibilities for all women.

All: We Pray for our daughters and granddaughters.
May they be granted the power to seek that life which is uniquely theirs.

continued

(Here add any women you would like to remember or for whom you wish to pray.)

All: We have celebrated the power of many women past and present. It is time now to celebrate ourselves. Within each of us is that same life and light and love. Within each of us lies the seed of power and glory.
Our bodies can touch with love; our hearts can heal; our minds can seek out faith and truth and justice.
Spirit of Life, be with us in our quest.
Amen.

ANN M. HEIDKAMP

Benedictions

God came down to us
like the sun at morning
wounded to the heart
by our helplessness.
Let us now depart
in his strength
to love and serve
one another.

★ ★ ★

The hands of the Father uphold you,
The hands of the Saviour enfold you,
The hands of the Spirit surround you,
And the blessing of God Almighty,
Father, Son and Holy Spirit
Uphold you evermore.
Amen.

★ ★ ★

Go in peace
and proclaim to the world
the wonderful works of God
who has brought you liberation.

We go forth in faith and hope
to love and to serve
secure in the knowledge
that God is with us always.

Deep peace of the running wave to you,
Deep peace of the flowing air to you,
Deep peace of the quiet earth to you,
Deep peace of the shining stars to you,
Deep peace of the Son of peace to you.

Iona Community

★   ★   ★

The blessing of the God of Sarah and Abraham,
The blessing of the Son, born of Mary,
The blessing of the Holy Spirit who broods over us
as a mother over her children
be with you all.

JANET MORLEY

For Travellers

May the road rise up to meet you.
May the wind be always at your back.
May the sun shine warm upon your face,
the rains fall soft upon your fields
and until we meet again,
may God hold you in the palm of His hand.

Traditional Celtic blessing

Disclosure

Prayer is like watching
for the kingfisher.
All you can do is
Be where he is likely to appear
And wait.
Often, nothing much happens:
There is space, silence
And expectancy.
No visible sign.
Only the Knowledge
That He's been there
And may come again.
Seeing or not seeing cease to matter,
You have been prepared.
But sometimes when you've almost
Stopped expecting it,
A flash of brightness
Gives encouragement.

ANN LEWIN

Acknowledgements

BARROWBY, 'Before Birth: A Waiting Prayer' and 'Birthday Prayer' unpublished. Copyright Barrowby. Printed by permission of Barrowby.

CAPEL, Evelyn Francis, 'Trinity', 'Ephiphany', 'Advent', 'Lent' and 'Whitsun' from *Prayers and Verses for Contemplation*, published by Floris Books. Copyright Floris Books. Reprinted by permission of Floris Books.

CASSIDY, Sheila, 'Forgiveness', 'Daring to Believe', and 'Send Us Out' from *Good Friday People*, published by Darton Longman & Todd Ltd, and Orbis Books. Copyright Darton Longman & Todd Ltd. Reprinted by permission of Darton Longman & Todd Ltd.

FARRELL, Maureen FCJ, 'In This Place', unpublished. Copyright Maureen Farrell. Printed by permission of Maureen Farrell.

GALLOWAY, Kathy, 'Out of the Depths' from *Celebrating Women*, published by The Movement for the Ordination of Women. Copyright Kathy Galloway. Reprinted by permission of Kathy Galloway.

GARNER, Heather, 'God of Fire, God of Light'. Copyright Heather Garner. Reprinted with permission from Heather Garner.

GNANADASON, Aruna, 'The Power of Hope' from *Your Will Be Done*, edited by Alison O'Grady, published by CCA Youth Desk 1984.

Anna McKenzie. Reprinted by permission of Anna McKenzie.

MURRAY, Shirley, 'The Birth of Jesus' from *The Bible Through Asian Eyes*, published by Pace Publishers and Consultant Editors. Copyright Pace Publishers and Consultant Editors. Reprinted by permission of Pace Publishers and Consultant Editors.

RATUSHINSKAYA, Irina, 'A Little Song' from *Pencil Letter*, published by Bloodaxe Books. Copyright Irina Ratushinskaya. Reprinted by permission of Bloodaxe Books.

REBERA, Ranjini, 'The Sinful Woman' and 'Miriam's Song' from *The Bible Through Asian Eyes*, published by Pace Publishers and Editors. Reprinted by permission of Pace Publishers and Consultant Editors.

ROBERTSON, Jenny. 'Corn King' from *A Touch of Flame*, published by Lion Publishing. Copyright Jenny Robertson. Reprinted by permission of Jenny Robertson and Lion Publishing.

SÖLLE, Dorothee, 'Wisdom of the Indians' from *Of War and Love* by Dorothee Sölle. Translated from the German by Rita and Robert Kimber. English translation copyright © 1983 Orbis Books, Maryknoll, NY 10545, printed with permission of Orbis Books.

TAYLOR, Bridgette, 'Beauty for Ashes?' and 'You Say You Know', unpublished. Copyright Bridgette Taylor. Printed by permission of Bridgette Taylor.

WHITE, Rowena Eldin, 'For He who Would Marry a Childless Woman' and 'Psalm 139 For Childless Women'. Copyright Rowena Eldin White. Reprinted by permission of Rowena Eldin White.

WILKIE, Ellen. 'Despite All' and 'Afraid' from *Pithy Poems*. Copyright

Estate of Ellen Wilkie. Reprinted by permission of Pauline and John Wilkie.

WORLD COUNCIL OF CHURCHES for permission to use 'By His Wounds You Have Been Healed' from *Women in a Changing World*, WCC Publications. Printed with permission.

ZUNDEL, Veronica. 'Song' from *Faith in Her Words*, edited by Veronica Zundel, published by Lion Publishing. Reprinted by permission of Lion Publishing.

Artwork *The Pietà* from *The Bible Through Asian Eyes*, published by Pace Publishers and Consultant Editors and reprinted with their permission.

Every effort has been made to trace the ownership of copyright items in this collection and to obtain permission for their use. The author and publisher would appreciate notification of, and copyright details for, any instances where further acknowledgement is due, so that adjustments may be made in a future reprint.

Index of First Lines of Prayers

Index of First Lines of Prayers ———————————————————— 179

Index of First Lines of Prayers ———————————————

Index of Authors